There is No Deadline

Elizabeth McRae

BookLeaf Publishing

Presentation by *BookLeaf Publishing*

Web: www.bookleafpub.com

E-mail: info@bookleafpub.com

ISBN: 9789357445368

First edition 2021

DEDICATION

To me. You finally did it.

Dip Me in Water

Scraped knees,
Gravel buried and bloodied
Calloused palms,
Rough skin, like a dry brush
Against and empty, silent canvas

Dip me in water

Take it in
Toothless smiles become full
Flowers aren't just for picking
The scents contagious
Spilling secrets one petal at a time,
She loves me… not?

Dip me in water

This time a shade darker
Indigo skyline across fresh skin
Now silky and soft with the loss
Of endless Indian summers

Foot and gravel
Elbow and concrete
Mind and sky

Now foot means forward
Elbow means push
Mind means future

Scraped knees?
Just remnants, silvery lines
Reminders

Dip me in water

Paint me across this once empty,
Silent canvas
And you'll see
How the acoustics
Lose their sounds, slippery
Slipping like a weak step
On the translucent surface
Of frozen life

Dip me in water

How soiled and muddied
Tainted as
Flowers meet bloodied knees
And chapped lips lose their once
Fearless shape

Dip me in water

Drag my once simple smile
And with a stroke,
See how each dunk, each soft sip
Both drinks and gives way
Empty no more
But no more full
Just keeping time

Until I am dipped again.

Forest Fire

smoke stings my throat as I inhale deeply
funny how I thought I would ever escape it
flames licking at my heels, my socks singed with black
crimson red blisters spread across my calves
thighs, stomach, arms, neck,
heart.

I wonder if I drew lines between them,
like a child using crayons on a breakfast diner menu
what shape would they make?

I'd like to think the connection between them
would be beautiful the way constellations are
...sparkling and fluid, a testament to time and strength

but i am not a child
...how i wish i was.

I want to dip my fingers in paint and smear it
across the dining room table

I want to make a mess and be able to wipe it
away with a baby wipe

instead I sit
engulfed in a forest fire
and the consequences that come with caring
the consequences that come
                                        the consequences

and now my skin is scorched
just like the redwoods that once kissed the sky

they used to remind me that it was okay to let
visitors trek

see the unseen
touch the untouched

but they were wrong to ever let someone step
foot in their home,
because now they are up in flames
and they took me with them.

my senses drowning in the scent of dying trees
and burning skin

this is no connect-the-dots
my life is far from a constellation

The Dark

When I go to bed, it's 9:23 P.M
I will my mind to quiet, my breaths to steady
And I welcome the heavy sensation of sleep,
lolling in the back of my tired eyes
I embrace it

When I wake up, it's 2:13 A.M.
My body soft, free of the hungry pain of tension
My lungs expand slowly as my eyelids flutter
open
Only to see perpetual darkness, only to hear the
raspy whispers of the night
Faintly I hear them... this is when my fear of the
dark began
As this ancient voice I learned,
is not your friend

By 3 A.M., I'm calling for sleep
I'm yelling its name, yearning for its light
embrace to come over and take me away
But the dark shouts louder, it words more
persuasive, its voice more deafening
And I'm left staring into its poisonous eyes
It brushes against my cheeks, murmuring
sweetly in my ears

But its presence causes a ghostly coldness to seep into my bones
My heart races and quickly speeds up
Until its sprinting, running across through the night
The long fingers of terror nipping close behind, scratching my heels

But I'm no match for the swift horror, I'm no match for the strength of night
And soon I'm in its clutches,
And I am forced to look straight into the vicious gaze of blackness
And bear witness to the reflection of my own terrified eyes
In them I see everything I've grown to fear
Everything

Losing my mom at the grocery store
Cracks of lightning and the deep vibration of thunder
Stomach-churning wreckage of cars and empty persons lying at my feet

But then it turns more hideous, it turns more cruel
And sleep is no longer in my grasp

What will you do when they realize? The dark whispers tauntingly.
What will you do when they realize you're actually a horrible ugly person? It purrs.

What will you do when they no longer see your flaws as endearing, but for what they are? Awful mistakes not being worth forgiven over.
What will you do when they realize that you are full of self-loathing and hate just like the rest of the world?
What will you do when they see that you are struggling to keep up? Struggling to move forward?
What will you do when they leave you behind?
What will you do when they cast you away?
What will you do?

You will be alone, dear girl. It says while caressing my face, piercing my heart.
You will be alone.

At 6 A.M., I wake.
But I am hesitant to move. I don't want to move.
As I long for sleep's gentle embrace.
Because I wasn't granted rest.
I wasn't granted rest.
No.
I was too afraid of the dark to sleep.

And if you're not afraid, if you're not fearful…
you should be.
Because there is a reason why everyone is
terrified of the dark.
You will find your reason soon enough.

Atlas

sometimes I glance up at the sky
my head tilted back, and I wonder...
does the sun ever get tired of being the center of
our galaxy?
i wonder, does rising every morning and setting
every night become a burden
the way waking up each day and going to sleep
each night is for me?
this can't possibly be true as i am not the center
of the universe
no one this weak ever could be

though I feel like I attract things the way the
warmth of the sun does
i can't control what's pulled into my
gravitational orbit
even though I try
in this, I have more in common with what is in
the sky
than I do with very beings I share my body with

I wonder what it's like to have the responsibility
of a star
to be relied on to always shine
to be there before and after

But I look down at the sand beneath my feet
And I know I do not have to look further than
my own person

I exist only to die
this truth is the same for
the celestial beings that
make up everything we know

So I gaze out into my orbit,
My chest heavy and full of star dust and silent
sobs
And see only reflections of myself: those who
don't see the cracks in their own skin,
tiny golden slivers of light peeking out,
little lines that suggest the existence of
something more than reality,
something under the surface of smiles and hearty
laughs

I stitch together these cracks
my hand is gentle,
this i know

is this how the sun feels?
providing a blanket for an entire galaxy?
a great provider, the ultimate healer
existing in spite of the inevitable end of time?

it shines into every crevice
never wavering
but how does it not tire?

it seems that's all I do
the struggle to peel back the sheets
to put my feet on the cold hardwood floor
to do it all over again,
to reach my hands out into the world
and catch whatever comes my way
to grasp them and hold them close to my heart

sometimes i feel like god made a mistake when
he made me
he gave me a finite amount of love, I am no star
how can I stitch the wounds of others
when I can barely do that for myself?

I am not celestial in any definition of the word
and the burden in knowing that weighs heavy on
my shoulders
I am no Atlas

I cannot sustain a lifetime of stitching and
sharing stardust
when it is all I have
but it's easier to do things alone
when that's all you've known

But I don't have to do this alone
I've spent too much time searching for meaning
in the transcendence of stars
Too much time thinking and grasping for
something beyond the blue sky
That I've forgotten that I am not supposed to be
made like the sun
I am flesh, blood, and bone
So maybe the sun grows tired day after day,
maybe it does not
But I am not the sun,
The only galaxy I have resting on my shoulders
is my own

It is easier to do things alone
When that's all you've known

We're made of flesh, blood, and bone
We're not celestial
The weight of our little worlds are heavy
We're not as strong as Atlas
And we don't have to be
because we can carry it together

Earth Always Wins

The cold is comforting
In a way it never has
Been before

For some reason, ice on
The streets
Reminds me
That nature outlasts all

I am nobody,
Yet this thought
Brings a smile to my face
As the harsh winter wind
Whips at my cheeks,

It's comforting,
Knowing that I am but a
Single drop of rain
In the storm that is
The universe

Because that means
The worry I have now
The suffering that spreads
Through me like wildfire

Over the yellow foothills
Of California
Won’t matter,
And never will

Not when temperatures change
And forests grow
Not when my body will be decomposing
Eighty years from
Now, spreading
And providing for
New life

It’s comforting
to
Know,
Earth always wins.

Burn

My dreams have crossed the bridge into reality
But why do they burn?
Black smoke meets heavy fog
Crashing together to forge one suffocating hand
That never seems to mind strangling my neck

Tomorrow all the stars
Will be aligned so perfectly,
but the flutter of the humming bird's wings
Will bring the all too familiar feeling of
Fire and empty breaths

Something vital is missing
Purification
Is no longer a function
Plucked from my body
Deemed dispensable by my deadly friend

Most definitely I am lacking a lung
Or maybe even two, as the ocean's salty air
Seeps into the torn flesh of my body
Stinging me free of life's great mysteries and
joys
Instead of the ancient reassurance I grew to
depend on

What has changed?
The will of fate plagues me with unease
As I screen myself for insanity
For an answer for why I no longer feel whole
Why it melts my mind
Lingering blisters

I'm too dangerous for safe
Too safe for dangerous
And I'm stuck speeding in the slow lane
When all I want to do is look out the passenger window
And see what it used to be

I want to know that I am lucky enough
To be left behind by my blaze of a shadow
To wake up every morning
And not feel a stranger
In my own skin

Rocks

like bones sunken into the earth
dirt and sweat collide
as I dig or perhaps bury
the rocks in my mind

roads between us
like stars from the skies
filth in my fingernails
from silencing my cries

what begins this sorrow
what ends its life
no surprises today, it was me
the choice, was mine

how the sun knows to rise
I knew my fate
nevertheless it happened
and the fork was made

I saw before me
what was to come
but the river flowed anyway
and breath still entered my lungs

like bones sunken into the earth
it gently lays to die
even with my hands so close
it resists to close its eyes

even like prophecy from above
it didn't hurt any less
in the opening applause of the future
I choose instead to make the mess

the rocks of my mind
my fear of within
caged like an animal
kept me from peering in

and now the burden
is too much to bear
though I knew it was coming
I knew I would care

like bones sunken into the earth
it seeps deeper and deeper into my chest
I brought this upon myself
my rocks will never rest

It's Funny

It is funny how the heart races,
both in the good and the bad
Tell me,
Why does love stir just as much as pain?

I guess that's the point of it all
To walk across the bridge
and stop in the middle

From your stance in equilibrium,
like yin and yang
rocks and sand
good and bad
love and pain

It is the point of it all
that is for sure

but what happens
when your foot takes a heavy step
on the worn down wood

and you're suddenly
on the other side

what then?
will I ever know which side I crossed to?

A Different Lens

there is a moment
before your finger moves to click
where you remember where you are
because you've been living, it seems
somewhere else, outside the frame.

you had, for awhile,
stopped being in this world
caught tip-toeing on just a facet
because a closer look
would mean shifting weight
past the one-dimensional
and into the crevices that at first glance
felt too shallow to ever mean anything real

its funny how lighting changes things
how the lens rests on top of your cheek
a familiar pressure that seems to
only affirm the otherness
of being on the other side

and through this tunnel view
you lose sight of the warm blue blanket sky
and are subjected to observe
as you had always done

a witness to the dissonance
of a
short
second
of stillness
the timelessness of humanity
but for you, it took more than time

you realize after the flash
the moment melting into the whisper of the
breeze
not that the image is false
but the relation is false

you see again, on this side
how close everything is
to every other thing

how close you are to everything

so why do you insist on
just being a face behind the lens?

Pinky-Promise

sweet talk of memories
old joys, previous thrills
enough to keep the conversation
that is our relationship going on forever
but what if that is all it is?
reflections of our young selves
one continuous look into the ever-still pool of
our past…
nothing but forgotten experiences keeping us
together
the ones that are forgotten until the present no
longer pleases
is this small talk real? or just a formality?
the word friend escapes your lips
i had almost forgotten, of course
we were still friends in your eyes, in mine too
but not in my heart,
the veins of my body are much smarter and more
intelligent than my mind

we were friends
friends make sacrifices for each other
reach out across the stormy seas for one another
know each other better than the back of one's
own hands

maybe you knew you could forget me because
i'd never leave
because how could i forsake everything we
have?

but time has sobered me up, i've opened my
eyes....
i've always regarded time has a healer
but i'm afraid it will never heal us
it will never heal me

but hey, i get it now,
i see you
someone who didn't keep their pinky-promise...
and i see me
someone who so badly wanted to
and thanks to you,
i don't think i'll make one ever again

Ode to the Human Body

Sharp edges harmonize with lines so soft
Reflections show one single way to see
Our veins do storm and thunder as they ought
Your curves sketch beauty like the ocean deep

Within your face you see a harsh like form
But see the snow capped mountain fractures white
Like canvas lines your skin is stretched and torn
In that the swirling river eddies light

In blossoms of your stomach, breast, and waist
The moon goes round the planet that is you
Deep in your beating heart, you breed self hate
But glaciers, tigers make that shame untrue

As stars, your brothers, forest glades your friends
Where nature starts, the beauty does not end

Jumping the Fence

What is this besides
jumping the wooden fence
of the backyard of solitude
into the destitute and ragged
property of company?

chased from one to the other
as the cops of our mind
race after our thoughts, scaring us
like underage high schoolers at a party

a constant struggle,
tension of being torn
while the doubt makes a force
so strong its hard to fight
my body too weak to hit

so instead
I find myself
sprinting toward
the wooden fence
that always seems to leave splinters on
my fingers

and once again
I've crossed the boundary
of people into seclusion

All because of an instinct
that tells me that
something
is not right,
strange,
an imbalance

but why?
I wonder as I leverage myself up
why do my thoughts betray me?

and I realize...
its so nobody else can

I Witnessed Crimson

Gazing out the window, the sun shining bright

I look at the colorful cars speeding by

But then I feel my heart fold into my chest

As uniforms gather round as I witness

Across the way, a circle of cars
And through the cracks, I see an arm

Folding a white sheet stained with crimson
The form of a body, unmoving and frozen

No other vehicles, cars, or persons
Just the white sheet stained with crimson

A gasp leaves my quivering lips
As my heart speeds up, stirs, and skips

I'm unable to tear my gaze away
From where the darkened cloth lay stained

What had happened? Who had been hit?
Who was the person who no longer existed?

What was wrong? Why did she die?
Later that night, I found out it was a suicide

A girl who was hurt and broken beyond repair
Walked across a six-lane highway out of deep
despair

Her picture smiling cheerfully on the screen
My vision turns blurry after recalling what I had
seen

The image of the sheet blossomed with red
For awhile was the only thing circling in my
head

Why had this happened? Why did she die?
Why did she choose death over life?

I always knew why, I always knew the answer
As devastation and sadness spread faster than
cancer

As its ghostly and hateful cells stayed concealed
Not all broken hearts can be healed

And every time I see the crimson sheet in my mind
I remember that the world will never completely be fine

Because that joyful girl no longer breathes
Never again will she dance or sing
Never again will love happily
Because now, she lay cold and still on the site of her death scene
Underneath the red blossoms of the crimson stained sheet

Bubbly

I wanted it to be real
but how many times had I felt
the bubbly against my lips
mistaking the bitter taste for complexity
instead of a facade for vanilla insecurity

Tangerine Sweet

tangerine sweetness
filters my vision

swinging, not dangling
flying over the edge
rapid water slows into still

to inhale
and not feel a single
weight on my chest

how i wish to dig
my fingers into the orange skin
of a tangerine

my biggest worry:
accidentally swallowing a seed

and growing a fruit tree in my stomach

Five Feet Under

What more can I do?
to nurture, to offer every ounce
every sliver
of myself

always try your best, they'd say
work now, play later
as if the flowers waited to bloom
the sun waited to shine

What more can I do?
what more can I do than give away my ever
growing glass heart
its chipped pieces here and there
in the crevices in my past,
but mostly
in the clouds of my future

What more can I give than everything I have?

It will come soon and bring the euphoria of life
you've been lucky to see in the tiny
slits in the window shade
soon you'll be outside
you just wait, dear

you'll see
learn
and believe

yeah, I say
but someday,
I'll be five feet under too

Her

I turn the corner,
my breath speeds up with each undulation
of my heart
I hear blood in my ears and feel earthquakes
in my chest

each fault line gives way to the other
unifying to create chaos in the body meant
to sustain me
a tumultuous life, a tumultuous death

my mind is an 8 on the Richter scale
breaking and succumbing
destroying

my organs follow its example
what else are they to do?
there is no cure for the stones in my throat
the earth in my lungs
no cure for collapse

I press my back against the brick wall behind
me,
desperate for some sensation to ground me

my eyes drop to my shadow as red fills my
cheeks
and I see

her

distorted and dark
an abstract version of reality but
still
here

she doesn't have the magnitude of my mind
surely it would kill her the way it almost kills
me

but she always seems to forget that she's a part
nature
in a way I am not
maybe that's why she's able to dance behind me,
keeping me company

she moves her elongated form
mimicking my own
her arms stretch farther than mine across
the black concrete that burns underneath the
soles we share

the tremors are
so

loud

I bring a hand to my mouth to stifle a cry

and she?
she brings a hand to her mouth to stifle a laugh

there is no escape from natural disasters

Silence

Growing up I had a hard time sitting,
a hard time being
If I was given a body, why couldn't I move?
Why was I given a voice if I couldn't speak?

As a child, I never understood why
teachers wanted silence, how they'd count down
or why my mom hushed me to take a phone call

The world is full of sounds
I was young and the grass in my backyard spoke
in whispers to me
I shared secrets with the redwood trees
I had conversations with pill bugs

Never could I sleep in a silent room
Scratchy tunes, violins and oboes
the fear of the dark
Something to always fill the emptiness
Of the quiet night

To sit in silence, would be to let things in
The cries of dogs, the speeding of cars
The chatter of the monsters under my bed

even now, there is an impulse to drown things
out
to fill the unknown with something
rather than accept the nothing

but as I sit here,
scratching at my skin, picking at my fingers, my
leg bouncing with uneasiness
I see you

following the familiar flow of silence, the
presence of the infinite
you move like you are more than an
acquaintance
with the idea of listening, of sitting,
of breathing
existing so naturally in a space I've always been
terrified of

you squeeze my hand
slowly repainting the canvas of my mind,
one car ride, one stoplight, one inhale at a time

silence isn't as scary anymore
From your stance in equilibrium,
like yin and yang
rocks and sand
good and bad
love and pain

It is the point of it all
that is for sure

but what happens
when your foot takes a heavy step
on the worn down wood

and you're suddenly
on the other side

what then?
will I ever know which side I crossed to?

www.ingramcontent.com/pod-product-compliance
Lightning Source LLC
Chambersburg PA
CBHW051743130826
49812CB00033B/979
9789357445368